What are we learning?

What will we learn this week?

New Words

We will learn lots of **words about places**, SOME of the words we will learn are on the next page, but we will learn many more.

Questions (and answers)

We will learn to ask **Is he/she at...** We will learn about contractions

More Questions (and answers)

We will learn to ask **Where is he/she** and **Where are they.** We will review the difference between he, she and they.

Grammar

We will learn about **prepositions.** For example: on, next to and under. We will also learn about **articles** and when to use (and not use) them.

Phonics

We will learn about the **magic e**. A special letter that when you put it at the end of a word changes the sound of the vowel.

Spelling

We will learn how to spell some of the words we learnt

And Fun!

We will also play lots of games and have lots of fun!

Learn Some Words

Question Time

Is he at the park?

No, he is not.

Is he at the beach?

Yes, he is.

Where is he?

He is at the beach.

Ask and answer

Is he at the hospital? Is she at the beach? Where is he?

Can you do it?

Ask one classmate to stand on a flashcard and then ask,

Where's he? or **Where's she?**

Who can answer the most questions?

Let's match

Ask the question, where is he? Or where is she? And then match up the sentences with the pictures

He's at the beach

She's at the park

She's at the ______________

She's at the _____

He's at home

Let's Draw

Draw a picture of a girl or a boy somewhere, then write, where are they?

More Words

Let's learn some places. Draw the pictures of the words you learned here:

Do you know what these places are?

Swimming pool
Shopping mall
Supermarket
Book shop
Toy shop
Restaurant
Hotel
Gas station

What else do you know?

Now your teacher is going to play a game with you with these words – but only if you can jump!

Have Some Fun

Play memory – your teacher is going to put the cards face down, let's see if you can remember where you are! Write the words you got here:

____

____

More Questions

Where**'s she**?

Where**'s he**?

Where **are they**?

Ask and answer

Where's she?	Where's he?	Where are they?

Can you do it?

Draw a picture in the box. Then challenge your classmates to guess what you have drawn.

Let's write

	Where's she?	______________________ ______________________
	Where are they?	______________________ ______________________
	____________ __________ __________ __________?	______________________ ______________________
	____________ __________ __________ __________?	______________________ ______________________
	____________ __________ __________ __________?	______________________ ______________________

Have some fun!

On a separate piece of paper write a question and answer. Then cut it up and challenge your friend to put it back together. When you are finished paste your sentence here.

Grammar

Where are you?

Practice Time!

Look at the word and see if you can draw a picture to match

on	
next to	
under	
behind	

Have some fun!

Can you run? Your teacher will put lots of pictures on the floor and then will call out a word. You have to run to find the right one!

When you are finished write down all the words you got here:

More fun

Let's play a silly game. Listen to your teacher. He will say a word. You follow the word. For example if he says 'ON' then stand ON your chair!

Phonics

Let's learn about the Magic E!

The magic e can change the sound of o

Try reading this word.

hom_

Now put an 'e' on the end and see how it changes the sound

Practice

Using the alphabet cards make a three letter word with an 'o' in the middle.

Then put a magic e on the end and see how it changes. Write the words you made here:

____

____

Practice

Word Wheel

Cut out the shapes on the next page and attach them to this page
How many words can you make? Write them here

•

make
words
here

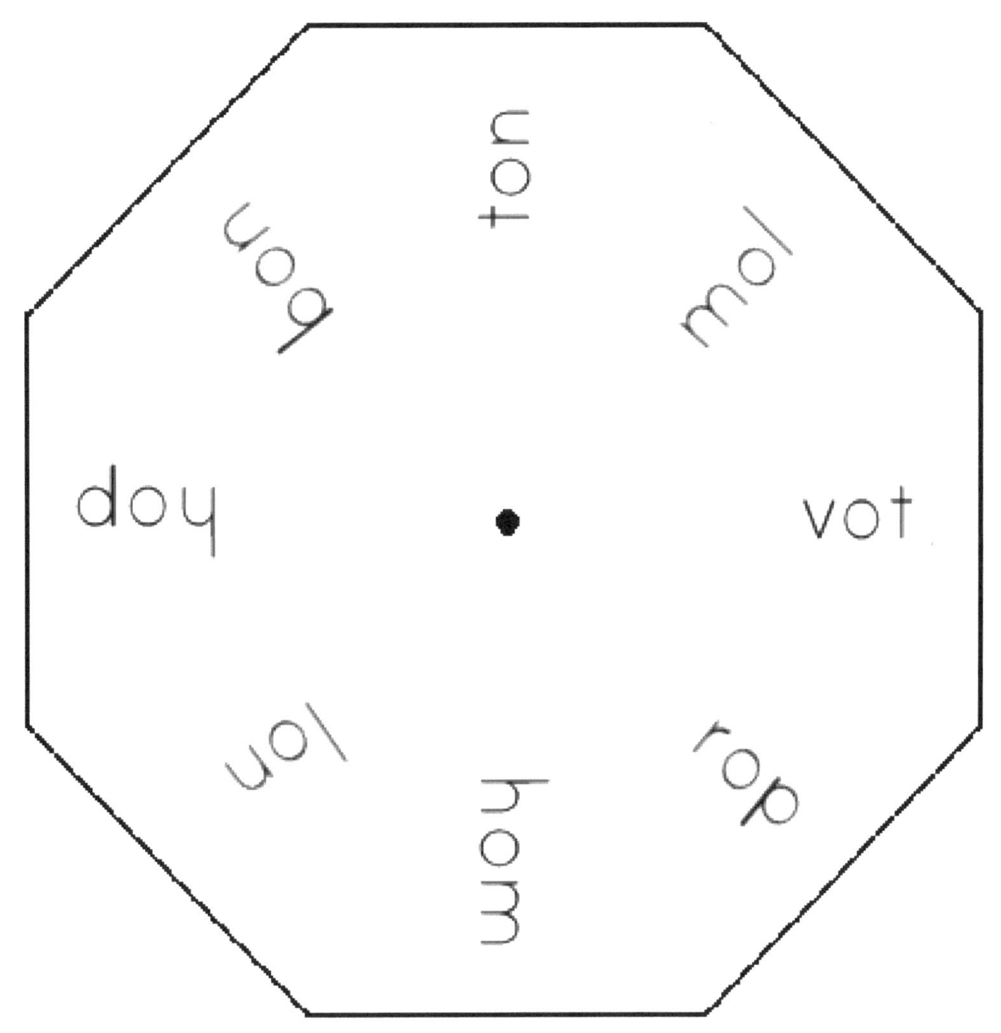

e

Daily English

Useful verbs at home

study English

talk on the telephone

watch TV

practice the piano

Have some fun!

Play Pictionary! Draw a word on the whiteboard and see if anyone can guess what you are drawing.

Spelling

Let's practice the words! Please LOOK, COVER, WRITE and CHECK every day!

	Monday	Tuesday	Wednesday	Thursday
school				
home				
shoe store				
_____ store				
park				
zoo				
beach				
hospital				

Phonics (2)

The magic e can also change the other vowels, a e i o and u

Try reading these:

Cat_

Pet_

Win_

Hom_

Hug_

Now add a magic e to the end and see how they have changed

Read

Read a story! You are going to read a story called, 'Nine White Mice' – a funny story about a lot of mice and a very bad cake!

Let's practice!

Two words

Read the words below. Then cut of the magic e and put it at the end of each word – can you read it now?

Hop

Cub

Win

Kit

Mak

Pet

Now listen to your teacher, he is going to say a word – FAST – who can make the words the fastest?

Homework (1)

Homework (2)

How many words can you find? Write them below.

F	M	Q	O	F	X	S	H	O	P	P	I	N	G	G
L	C	O	U	N	F	A	A	T	I	V	O	V	K	W
O	E	C	A	M	W	S	O	Y	Z	V	K	B	M	S
O	E	T	S	U	P	E	R	M	A	R	K	E	T	E
P	P	H	O	S	P	I	T	A	L	Q	T	Q	O	K
P	F	D	Z	H	S	W	I	M	M	I	N	G	U	E
K	A	O	B	C	G	A	S	A	R	T	C	X	D	D
X	O	B	E	A	C	H	Z	L	L	H	E	S	M	K
R	E	S	T	A	U	R	A	N	T	O	T	X	Q	H
P	K	K	S	H	L	J	W	J	E	A	O	R	R	K
P	Q	N	J	Y	L	D	C	B	T	M	K	H	I	E
A	T	D	O	Q	A	P	O	I	B	S	O	R	C	Y
R	H	T	H	Y	M	O	O	D	J	Z	J	H	Z	S
K	R	O	W	C	K	N	Z	H	Y	A	R	B	I	L
O	D	E	R	H	I	C	F	M	S	C	Y	J	U	H

Have some fun!

You've worked hard, now it is time to have some fun! We are going to make a town! When you are finished take a photo and stick it here:

More writing

If you need any more space to write, then use these pages

Don't loose them!

Put your mini flashcards here once you have cut them out

Mini Flashcards

at school	at home
at the ____ shop	at the shoe shop
at the park	at the zoo
at the hospital	at the beach

Completion of
Mark's Mad Holiday
This certificate is presented to
for completing the 'places' unit
BUS 10
SCHOOL
Crayons

www.ingramcontent.com/pod-product-compliance
Ingram Content Group UK Ltd.
Pitfield, Milton Keynes, MK11 3LW, UK
UKHW060122300726
14090UKWH00002B/315